P9-CMA-348

BLAIRSVILLE SENIOR HIGH SCHOOL
BLAIRSVILLE, PENNA.

RACE CAR LEGENDS

The Allisons

Mario Andretti

Crashes & Collisions

Drag Racing

Dale Earnhardt

Formula One Racing

A.J. Foyt

Jeff Gordon

Motorcycles

Richard Petty

The Unsers

Women in Racing

CHELSEA HOUSE PUBLISHERS

T 25871

Chelsea House 98-99 $

RACE CAR LEGENDS

CRASHES & COLLISIONS

Michael Benson

CHELSEA HOUSE PUBLISHERS
Philadelphia

Produced by Daniel Bial and Associates
New York, New York

Picture research by Alan Gottlieb
Cover illustration and design by Robert Gerson
Cover photo credit: AP/Wide World Photos

Copyright © 1997 by Chelsea House Publishers, a division of Main Line Book
Co. All rights reserved. Printed and bound in the United States of America.

First Printing

1 3 5 7 9 8 6 4 2

Library of Congress Cataloging-in-Publication Data

Benston, Michael.
    Crashes & collisions / Michael Benson.
        p.   cm. -- (Race car legends)
    Includes bibiliographical references and index.
    ISBN 0-7910-4435-1
    1. Automobile racing--United States--History. 2. Automobile
racing drivers--United States--Biography.
[1. Automobile racing.   2. Automobile racing drivers.] I.
Title. II. Title: Crashes and
collisions.   III. Series.
GV1033.845   1997
796.72'0973--dc21
[B]   97-690
                                                        CIP
                                                        AC

Frontispiece photo: Some of the 12 cars involved in a collision at the fourth
turn of the 1966 U.S. 500.

CONTENTS

IT HAPPENS IN
A SPLIT SECOND

For auto racing fans, it is not just the speed that draws them by the hundreds of thousands every week to tracks all around the world. It is also the danger.

No other sport offers the chance of instant disaster quite the same way as auto racing. At any second, cars traveling at 200 mph might go out of control, their drivers all but helpless inside.

Race car drivers will tell you that they do not fear crashes and collisions on the track. Here's news for you: They lie! Every driver is well aware of what might happen if they make the smallest mistake.

One second they are in complete control, threading the needle again and again with their powerful machine. The next second, there is chaos. Perhaps a tire went flat and they are unable to steer. Maybe another car nudged them in the rear just enough to send them flying wildly toward a concrete wall. Whatever it is, it happens in a split second, and once the driver has lost control, he is simply along for the ride. Fate takes over.

Drivers know that a career-ending—or even a life-ending—injury could be right around the next turn. It's just that they are brave men and women, who accept the risks as a trade for the thrill of going fast.

This sequence of events from the 1939 running of the Indianapolis 500 shows how little time drivers have to adjust for potential crashes. In the top picture, Bob Swanson's car is out of control and on fire; another car narrowly avoids tragedy on the far side. Seconds later, in the middle photo, Floyd Roberts smashes into Swanson, throwing Swanson from his car. Swanson was injured, but not severely; Roberts died a short time later. Seconds later again, in the bottom photo, Chet Miller has also smashed into the wreckage. He too would survive, though his racing was done for the day.

Driving skill is important in avoiding accidents, but even the best drivers have had their run-ins with fate. At the 1988 Daytona 500, air got under the car of Richard Petty, widely acknowledged as the greatest stock-car driver ever. In one of the most dramatic accidents of all time, his car flipped over seven times. And when the car finally came to land on the track, it ended up directly in front of Brett Bodine, who had no chance to avoid Petty or even slow down. He piled into what was left of Petty's car at 180 mph.

Most people in the crowd feared that if Petty hadn't died while his car was barrel-rolling, he must have died when Bodine piled into him. Somehow, though, Petty had survived, and he wasn't even severely injured. He had a fractured shoulder and a bruised ankle, but only two days later, he was able to make an appearance—walking with a slight limp—on the television show, "Late Night with David Letterman."

After he retired, Petty couldn't even remember the number of ribs he had broken. He did figure that he had broken two dozen bones in various accidents and also had incurred permanent hearing loss from the years of listening to the loud roar of the engines.

Some families have been hit hard in the tragedies of racing. Bobby and Donnie Allison were great stock-car drivers during the 1970s and 1980s. In 1981, Donnie had to retire due to head injuries he sustained in a crash, and in 1988, his brother nearly died and was permanently injured in a crash. Donnie's son Cliff died in a 1992 accident. And Bobby's son, Dave, had established himself as a racing star too when he died trying to land a helicopter at the Talladega Superspeedway.

Bobby Unser has won three Indianapolis 500s; brother Al, Sr., has won four, and Al's son, Al, Jr., has won two. However, this family has also met with tragedy—Joe Unser, the uncle of Bobby and Al, Sr., was killed while practicing for the 1929 Indianapolis 500. Bobby and Al's brother, Jerry Unser, Jr., also died while practicing for the 1959 Indy 500.

Here are some of the most famous crashes and collisions in auto racing history, from 1909 to the present. Some drivers lost their lives. Others had their Guardian Angel riding shotgun and walked away. Some were badly injured, yet fought to get better so that they could race again.

And so we dedicate this book to Mark Donahue, Jimmy Clark, Bill Vukovich, Eddie Sachs, Dave McDonald, Fireball Roberts, Ayrton Senna, Ronnie Peterson, Neil Bonnett, Swede Savage, and the hundreds of other drivers who have made the ultimate sacrifice on the track—all so that we, the fans, can continue to enjoy the thrill of the speed—and the danger.

EARLY INDY DAYS

The Races of 1909 and 1911

For more than 80 years now, auto racers have been having a tough time driving their cars all the way around the 2½-mile Indianapolis Motor Speedway without hitting the walls. The Brickyard—so called because for many years its racing surface was made of bricks—has taken the lives of more drivers than any other race track in the world. The most recent tragedy came in 1996, when Scott Brayton hit the wall during practice.

Built in 1909, Indy was designed for a slower time. Cars at that time sped along at only one third of today's speeds. The track is narrow and it is a quadrangle rather than an oval. Rather than the long, easy curves of the modern super-speedway ovals, all four corners at Indy are very sharp. Two of the curves follow long stretches of

At the start of the first race at Indianapolis in 1909, drivers had to hand crank their engines in order to start them. At the left is the number three Knox car. Driver Urefrid Borque and mechanic Harry Holcombe both died in a crash during this race.

straightaway, so the cars enter the sharp left turn just as they have built up the most momentum. That means that the car will want to go straight, no matter how much the racer turns the steering wheel.

Modern racing ovals have turns that are steeply banked, tilted upward so the cars appear to be racing along the sides of a bowl. The banking helps to keep the car on the track. The corners at Indianapolis are almost flat. The racers must defy the laws of science just to keep their fragile machines on the racing surface—and away from disaster.

Still, Indy isn't nearly as dangerous as it was when it opened. The track in 1909 was like the surface of the moon compared to the silky smooth blacktop-and-cement surface drivers race on today. Even the bricks hadn't yet been put down. Made of dirt and crushed stone, the track back then tended to develop ruts in the "groove," the most-used lane on the track. It was so dusty during races, drivers had trouble seeing where they were going. To cut down on the dust, every once in a while the track would be oiled and tarred. A creek ran across the track, and the drivers had to cross a small bridge. The stands were small and wooden, compared to today's stadium, which is the world's largest grandstand.

When the Speedway first opened, the tradition of the Indy 500 each Memorial Day was unknown. The very first auto race at Indy came on August 20, 1909—not in the month of May at all. It was a 250-mile affair for 1908- and 1909-model stock cars. In the first of several races scheduled for the week as part of an "Auto Carnival," the winner got the "Prest-O Lite Trophy" and $1,000. The 10,000 fans in the stands did not have to wait long to see Indy's first bad crash. Drivers were only 60 laps into that very first race when disaster struck.

Driver Urefrid Borque, 29, and his mechanic Harry Holcombe were riding in second place in the Knox Car #3. (In those days, another man always rode in the car to help in case it broke down, and to look back to check for traffic.)

Borque had just passed the grandstand on the front stretch. Frank Brandoer of the Indiana National Guard was watching the race along the front straightaway, and the whole thing happened right in front of him. Something made both men in car #3 look back, Private Brandoer said. Borque took both hands from the steering wheel and threw his arms into the air, with a gesture that said, "There is nothing I can do." Then the car left the track.

In 1909, there were no concrete walls between the track and the fans—only fences. The Knox Car crashed through the fence and turned over, pinning both the driver and the mechanic underneath. No fans were hurt in the accident, but, in a second, hundreds of fans crushed forward to see or help. Borque died at the scene. Holcombe died just before arriving at the hospital. One of the rear wheels from the Knox Car #3 was found a few hundred feet from the crash. Maybe the wheel coming off had caused the crash. Perhaps the "axle nuts" had not been tightened properly during the car's last pit stop. No one would ever be sure.

After the crash, the race continued, but all of the Knox cars' drivers took themselves out of the race, out of respect for their fallen teammates. Within minutes of the crash, hundreds of spectators left the stands and headed home.

The deaths of Borque and Holcolme caused the organization that ran the race, the American Automobile Association (AAA), to make several demands to the owners of the track. All ruts had to be smoothed, and the entire track had to be oiled to keep down dust, instead of just the section in front of the grandstand.

The changes were made, but as it turned out, they didn't do much good. On August 22, 1909, only two days later, another fatal crash occurred. During a 300-mile race, a driver named Merz was piloting a National car along with mechanic Claude Kellum. The car's right front tire blew just as the car was about to cross the small bridge that spanned the stream. The car hit the bridge, flew up into the air, and then crashed through the fence, killing two members of the crowd. The car turned over, trapping Merz underneath. Merz was not seriously injured but Kellum was thrown against the fence when the car crashed through it, his head striking a post. He was rushed to the hospital but died an hour later. The accident started a stampede in the crowd, and two more fans were injured when they were trampled.

Fate had it in for Kellum that day. He didn't even start the race in the Merz car, but rather in a teammate's car. Kellum's original car broke down, so when Merz's mechanic tired himself out running to the pit area to get a new battery, Kellum volunteered to run the battery back to the doomed car.

A second accident, which seriously injured driver Bruce Keene, caused AAA officials to stop the race. The car struck the side of the bridge opposite the bleachers, and, though the car was

not severely wrecked, Keene suffered a serious cut on his head.

There would be no more racing at the Speedway again until Memorial Day 1911, when 80,000 fans watched the first Indy 500. This time, tragedy struck only 13 laps into the event when Arthur Greiner's Amplex threw a wheel and sent the car careening out of control, bucking like a bronco, on the backstretch. Greiner and mechanic Samuel Dickson were thrown into the air. Greiner suffered a concussion and a broken arm. Dickson was hurled into a fence and killed instantly. The crowd swarmed to the scene

In 1911, Ray Harroun won the first Indianapolis 500. His Morman Wasp averaged 75 miles an hour and featured the first rear-view mirror.

and pushed in so close that the driver and mechanic were trampled. Soldiers moved in and clubbed fans with their rifle butts to clear a path for doctors and an ambulance.

The other serious accident of the afternoon came about when Joe Jagerberger's Case broke a steering mechanism and began to spin down the front stretch. Mechanic C. L. Anderson was thrown out and Harry Knight swerved his Westcott to avoid hitting him. The Westcott then crashed into Herbert Lytle's Apperson which was parked in the pits. This contact sent the Westcott flying through the air and it came down on a parked Fiat.

This time the security people made sure that attempts to get doctors to the scene would not be slowed by the frenzied crowd, so guards on horseback formed a circle around the wreckage and injured men.

The commotion was such that the scorers at the start-finish line were unsure about which cars had passed, leaving the question of who

The attraction of breakneck speed and daredevil risk taking can be seen in this advertising poster from around 1910.

really won the race forever in dispute. The record books report, however, that Ray Harroun won the race in his Marmon Wasp with an average speed of 74.602 mph. His was the only one-seater car in the race.

The Wasp also contributed a major innovation to the automotive industry. Since Harroun had no mechanic to watch traffic, the Wasp was the first car ever to have a rear-view mirror.

2

VINTAGE BRICKYARD MAYHEM

Legendary crashes from the early days of the Brickyard

During the first 50 years of the Indy 500, there were many crashes—some tragic and some miraculous—that have become folklore in the history of auto racing. In 1914, for example, Ray Gilhooley had the most spectacular incident of the day, spinning wildly. The spin became so famous at the time that all spins for a while were known as "Gilhooleys."

The 1927 race featured a moment of heroics that is still talked about by fans who visit the classic racetrack each May. It involved driver Norman Batten, whose Miller car burst into flames on the front stretch on his 24th lap. Batten could have driven into the pits where there might have been a huge gasoline explosion. Instead, he bravely stood in the cockpit, flames licking up at his backside, and drove past the pits. He made sure that he had aimed the car

Smoke comes from the car of Bill Vukovich. Ed Elisian is in car number 68 (left) and Johnny Boyd is in number 39 (right). Vukovich died in the crash.

harmlessly toward the grass infield before he leapt to safety.

In 1930, there was a huge multi-car crash soon after the start. Since the crash appeared in newsreels, it soon became stock footage and was repeatedly used in Hollywood car-racing movies.

The Indy 500 lost a defending champion on the track for the first time in 1939 when Floyd Roberts was killed on lap 109 in a three-car accident that also sent drivers Bob Swanson and Chet Miller to the hospital.

In 1941, Wilbur Shaw's hopes of winning the race for a third time were dashed on lap 151 when a blown tire caused him to crash. The accident was blamed on a crew member, who shouldn't have used the tire as it was marked "no good."

Duke Nalon, driving a lightning-quick Novi in the 1949 race, broke a rear axle on the 24th lap. His gas tank exploded when he hit the wall, causing a curtain of flame to burn across the track. Some of the cars driving behind the accident were forced to drive right through the flame. Nalon's Novi was completely covered by the fire. He managed to hop out of the car soon after it came to a stop, so, although he suffered severe burns, his injuries were not bad enough to keep him out of the following year's 500.

May 30, 1955, was one of the darkest days in the history of Indy. Bill Vukovich, 36, defending two-time winner, was killed in an accident on lap 57. It was the second time that the defending winner was killed in the race.

Vukovich was in the lead, heading for his third straight victory, and racing down the backstretch, when cars he was about to lap spun out right in front of him. He plowed right into them and his Hopkins Special cartwheeled over the back wall and burst into flames. None of the other drivers were seriously hurt.

It was chilly (54°F) and windy that year at Indy. Many felt the weather caused the fatal accident. The incident began when Rodger Ward had his car caught by the steady 20 mph wind along the backstretch. Ward spun into the wall and his car turned end over end. Johnny Boyd and Al Keller tried to avoid the tumbling Ward and each smashed into the supports of a footbridge that then went over the backstretch. Ed Elisian plowed into this wreckage, completely blocking the track for Vukovich who was about two seconds behind.

Vukovich was speeding at about 150 mph when he hit. His car tumbled end over end over the outer wall and struck a safety patrol jeep sitting outside the track, slightly injuring two of its passengers. The race car then burst into flames. Fire trucks and safety crews were on the scene in less than a minute, but Vukovich was dead before he could be pulled from the car. The yellow caution lights around the track flashed on and the yellow flag was waved at the start-finish line. Fans around the track could see the smoke rising from behind the backstretch wall. Ten minutes after the crash, the crowd still had not been told which driver was in the burning car—although the track announcer did say that the incident was serious. Vukovich's wife, Esther, sat with the other drivers' wives near the start-finish line. She knew that Bill's car was not among those parading slowly around the track during the caution period. Mrs. Vukovich was then escorted to the hospital area where she was given the news.

Workers try to clear the wreckage after the worst accident in racing history. Pierre Levegh's Mercedes collided with another car, then caromed across the track and exploded into a stand of fans. This 1955 accident at Le Mans killed 88 people.

It was during that same year, 1955, that the worst accident in the history of car racing took place. It happened in Le Mans, France, on Sunday, June 12, during the running of the annual 24 Hours of Le Mans sports-car race. The tragedy happened when Frenchman Pierre Levegh's Mercedes hit another car, burst into flames, and flew over a dirt retaining wall into the tightly packed crowd. The accident killed 88 spectators and the driver, but the race went on. The wreck was so severe that President Dwight D.

Eisenhower said that auto racing should be banned in the U.S. Thankfully for us, nobody listened to Ike, safety measures improved, and the racing went on.

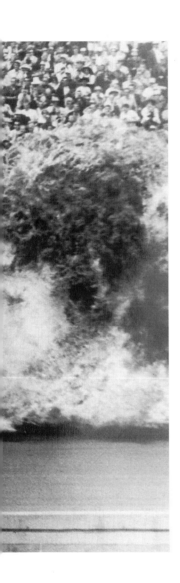

BLACK CLOUD OVER TURN FOUR

The 1964 Indianapolis 500

In auto racing, safety improvements are all-too-often inspired by tragedy. Such was the case when the rules for the Indy 500 were changed after the 1964 race. Gasoline was banned, and from that point on Indy cars have run only on a less explosive alcohol-based fuel.

As of 1964, there were no rules limiting the size of a car's gas tank, and many car builders made the tanks as big as possible to cut down on the number of pit stops they would need to go 500 miles. Most teams hoped to go the distance with only three pit stops. This meant two things: 1) the gas tanks were so heavy when full that they affected the balance of the car, and 2) the tanks were so big that, when full, the cars were like bombs waiting to go off.

Two drivers met their death in this blazing holocaust. Johnny Rutherford (number 86, left) managed to escape after being trapped briefly, and Ronnie Duman (number 64) also survived. But the popular Eddie Sachs and rookie Dave MacDonald perished during the running of the 1964 Indy 500.

25

The leaders of the race were finishing their second lap when one of the most horrifying crashes in auto-racing history occurred coming out of Turn Four at the top of the front stretch.

Rookie Dave McDonald of Riverside, California, driving the "Allstate Special," spun coming out of the turn and hit the inside wall. The car exploded into flames and drifted back onto the track. At that moment, long-time Indy favorite Eddie Sachs, of Detroit, Michigan, driving the American Red Ball Halibrand-Ford, smashed into McDonald and his car also exploded. Bobby Unser's, Johnny Rutherford's and Ronnie Duman's cars also caught fire.

As the cars smashed their way down the track spewing burning gas behind them, they spread the flames out until they covered the track. Unser managed to hop out of his car and roll around on the infield grass to put out the fire on his clothes. Rutherford escaped with mild burns. Duman would need to be hospitalized for weeks. Drivers Chuck Stevenson and Norm Hall also wrecked in the incident, but were uninjured.

Tom Sneva puts on a protective face covering after having suffered serious burns in an earlier race.

Huge clouds of billowing black smoke rose from the corner as emergency vehicles screamed onto the track. As many cars had to drive through the fire, the race was completely stopped (red-flagged). Sachs had died by the time they put out the fire and pulled him from his car. McDonald died 2 hours and 15 minutes later.

On the world-wide Indy 500 radio network, announcer Sid Collins gave an immediate tribute to Sachs: "Some men try to conquer life in a number of ways. In these days of our outer space attempts, some men try to conquer the universe. Race drivers are courageous men. They try to conquer life and death—and they try to calculate their risks. In our talking with them over the years, we have come to know their inner thoughts in regard to racing. They take it as a part of living. It is God's will, I'm sure, and we must accept that. We are all speeding toward death at a rate of 60 minutes every hour. The only difference is that we don't know how to speed faster—and Eddie Sachs did—Eddie Sachs exits the world in a race car."

The race was won by A. J. Foyt of Houston, Texas, in a Sheraton Thompson Watson Offenhauser car. His average speed was 147.350 mph, which was then the record.

Because of the tragedy, gasoline was banned at the Speedway. Starting the next year, no fuel other than methanol (wood-based alcohol) would be allowed. The new fuel, though flammable, did not explode when ignited the way gasoline did.

To show how the change in fuel, along with other safety improvements, have helped save the lives of Indy-Car drivers, only two drivers have been killed during Indy Car races since the 1964 accident.

In 1973, during the Indy 500, Swede Savage skidded out of control on the 58th lap, coming off of Turn Four not far from where the Sachs/McDonald crash had happened. His car turned sideways on the track before hitting the inside wall head-on. Savage was seriously injured with burns and broken legs, and later died in the hospital. Also killed in the incident was 22-year-old mechanic Armondo Teran, who jumped out of the pits to see what was happening and was struck by an emergency vehicle heading the wrong way up Pit Road.

Since then, the only other driver to be killed in an Indy Car race was rookie Jeff Krosnoff, who was driving his Reynard-Toyota in a race in Toronto in 1996. When his wheels touched the wheels of another car, he spun in the air like a helicopter, finally striking a fence helmet first. Also killed in the crash was track worker Greg Arvin, who was standing alongside the track and was struck on the head by one of Krosnoff's tires.

There have been plenty of spectacular crashes in the last 30 years at Indy that have not resulted in anyone getting killed. Sometimes that has been because of safety features in the car and on the track, and sometimes it has been because of blind luck. At the start of the 1973 race, the same year that Swede Savage had his fatal accident, the first attempt to start the race was marred by a horrible crash. Driver Salt Walther hit another car only a few hundred yards after taking the green flag. His car flew up into the "catch" fence that is supposed to protect the crowd. Many fans were injured when they were struck with flying metal and splashed with burn-

ing fuel. Walther was seriously burned, as he was trapped beneath his burning car when it finally came to a stop in Turn One.

The most memorable crash of the 1975 Indy 500 was Tom Sneva's fiery mishap in Turn Two. Sneva touched wheels with another car and went directly into the wall. His car exploded into many pieces and a huge flash of fire shot up from the car. Sneva, amazingly, walked away from the crash. It is believed that, if the accident had taken place 12 years earlier, Sneva would have been killed. Sneva had just made a pit stop when the accident occurred and his tank had been full of fuel. The tank, however, was a special, safe fuel system. The second the car made contact

Parnelli Jones dives out of his car when it catches fire in the pits during the 1964 Indy 500. Methane does not explode the way gasoline does. However, when it catches fire, its flames are nearly invisible.

Little of Stan Fox's car survived the crash with Eddy Cheever and the wall at the start of the 1995 Indy 500. Many will remember the sight of Fox's legs sticking out unprotected. Amazingly, Fox escaped the crash with his life.

with the wall, the tank pumped out its fuel. The tank held 40 gallons, but only 2½ remained in it when the wreckage was retrieved. The flames that flashed up from the accident were caused by the fuel that was still trapped in the lines.

Anyone who saw the 1995 running of the Indy 500 will never forget what happened to 42-year-old driver Stan Fox coming out of Turn One during the first lap. Fox, who started in the fourth row, had his inside tires touch what was called the "rumble strip," a bumpy ridge along the inside of the track meant to keep the drivers from cheating by cutting the corners too much. Fox's car veered right and went head-on into the outside wall. His car was then struck by one driven by Eddie Cheever, sending Fox into the wall again, this time helmet first. Cheever's car cut the front of Fox's car completely off, leaving Fox's legs dangling out of the car.

The eventual winner of that race, 24-year-old Jacques Villeneuve, had Fox on his mind even as he celebrated in Victory Lane.

"I am distressed that Stan was hurt because it's not something we like to see happen, but you run a risk as a driver," Villeneuve said. "My father died in a crash. Every driver lives life on the edge. We never think that we will hurt ourselves, but every driver is aware it might happen. Every driver, if he were not a racer, would probably be doing something else crazy. That's just the way we are."

Jacques's dad, Gilles Villeneuve, remains Canada's all-time greatest Grand Prix driver with six victories. He was killed in 1982 while practicing in a Ferrari for the Belgian Grand Prix. Jacques was 11 at the time.

As for Stan Fox, he survived his crash, although he remained unconscious for days. Amazingly, his legs were not injured. Today, Fox has almost completely recovered from his severely fractured skull and hopes one day to return to racing.

In 1996, when the green flag dropped to start the 1996 Indy 500, the rumble strip was gone.

MULTI-CAR PILEUPS

*The 1958 and 1966
Indianapolis 500s*

In the history of the Indy 500, several multi-car crashes at the start of the race have affected the outcome. Most memorably, it happened in 1958, with tragic consequences, and then again in 1966, this time with Lady Luck keeping a close eye on the drivers.

It was clear that there were going to be problems with the start of the 1958 race even before the flagman waved the green flag to officially start the competition. For some reason the front row passed the pace car and extra pace laps had to be held to get the field back in order, and even then the start was ragged.

There was still confusion among the drivers—the cars had fallen out of their three-by-three formation, as the 33-car pack roared nose-to-tailpipe through the first turn.

The crash started as the cars were entering the third turn on the first lap. The leader, Ed

*The famous first lap pileup at the 1966 Indy 500
begins. It was the biggest single accident at the
Brickyard since 1958's 13-car crash.*

33

Elisian, was attempting to pass Dick Rathmann on the inside when he lost control. Elisian was going about 170 mph when he got sideways and hit Rathmann. Pat O'Connor—an extremely popular 29-year-old local driver—was making his fifth start in the 500 when he hit this pile-up. O'Connor bounced off that first hit and then struck Jimmy Reece's car. This second collision caused O'Connor's car to flip upside down and catch fire.

The accident caused a chain reaction behind him. Jerry Unser—the brother of Indy superstars Bobby and Al Unser—struck Paul Goldsmith's car, ran over the top of Goldsmith's car, then cartwheeled down the track, over the outside wall and out of sight. Unser's crash looked a lot like Bill Vukovich's fatal 1955 crash, but Unser was a lot luckier. Unser escaped his journey with only a dislocated shoulder and a broken wrist. (Unfortunately, he was killed in a crash during practice at Indy two years later.)

O'Connor, on the other hand, was killed in the crash. The fatality prompted many of the estimated 200,000 people in the stands to head home, so the rest of the race was run before only partially-filled stands.

Thirteen cars were involved in the accident. Eight cars were out of the race, with many others so damaged that they limped along for the rest of the day. The yellow flag caused by the accident remained out for 29 minutes.

If such an accident had occurred at the start of an Indy 500 today, a red flag would no doubt have waved and the race would have been stopped until the track was cleared. But, back in 1958, the Indy officials were proud that the race had never been stopped for any other reason than weather. It was not until the 1964 crash

(see Chapter 3) that the first red flag for an accident was waved. As of 1996, there have only been four non-weather red flags at Indy. There were two red flags in 1973, one for the crash of Salt Walther and another for the fatal crash of Swede Savage. The fourth was caused by the Stan Fox crash in 1995.

Jimmy Bryan was one of only 14 cars still on the track at the end of the 1958 Indy when he won with an average speed of 133.791 mph. Bryan took advantage of the shrunken field and built up a lead of longer than a lap when he made his final pit stop. He was cruising when he took the checkered flag.

At the 1966 classic, the 50th running of the Indy 500, first-lap chaos again became the story of the day. This time, unlike the 1958 fiasco,

Cars continue to spin and collide with each other in the 1966 Indy 500 crash. Officials deemed the accident so severe, they stopped the race entirely to help the injured and clear debris.

there were no warnings during the pace laps that trouble lay ahead. Everything was running smoothly right up until the moment of disaster. The first two rows made it under the green flag without any problem. Behind that, there was big-time trouble. Canadian driver Billy Foster, who was starting in the fourth row, tried to squeeze between Gordon Johncock—who was supposed to start in the second row but had slipped back because he was having trouble getting his car up to speed—and the outer wall of Indy's main stretch. Before Foster could get there, the space disappeared, and he lost both of his right-side wheels against the wall. His car's nose cone was completely cut off by that first hit.

The nose cone got right in front of driver Mel Kenyon in the sixth row. Kenyon spun his car to get out of the way. That started the chain reaction—just like dominoes in a row. Car after car piled into the massive wreck.

Afterwards, Foster talked about the start of the accident. "There was an opening," he insisted. "I don't know who it was, but whoever was on my left moved up, and I had to swing out to avoid hitting him. Then someone bumped me in the right rear and I spun into the wall."

Huge Indy car tires bounced up and down the track. Torn sheet metal flew through the air. Debris from the accident even flew up over the catch fence and into the crowd.

Arnie Knepper, one of the drivers who never made it to Turn One, tried to explain what happened: "We all accelerated. Then there was a car up in the air and there were bits of wheels, radius rods, bits of metal. I almost made it. Then a car landed on me. A 1,400-pound auto can be pretty heavy when it's asittin' on your head."

Not all drivers were able to look at the crash with that kind of humor. Dan Gurney, whose Eagle was destroyed in the accident, was fuming with anger, and began to slam other drivers in the press as "having everything but brains." Gurney noted that "only an idiot" would think he could win a 500-mile race in the first 500 yards.

"Those clowns," Gurney fumed. "Ridiculous. I was hit four times out there. Four times! Wouldn't you think a bunch of grown men, all supposedly experienced race car drivers, could drive together down a simple stretch of straight road?"

While cars were already smashing together only a few hundred yards ahead, the flagman was still waving the green flag to the cars at the back of the field. The accident seemed to go on forever. And, even after the cars all came to a stop, those huge tires kept bouncing and bouncing.

A. J. Foyt's car got wrecked up against the outside wall near the stands. Instead of staying in his car and waiting to get hit again, Foyt got out of his car and climbed the fence in front of the stands.

One of the drivers from the middle of the pack who did get lucky enough to work their way through the accident without getting involved was European Grand Prix driving champion Graham Hill, from Great Britain, who was a rookie at Indy. "I was very fortunate," Hill said about the wild false start. "I just wandered in and out there and I made it through. Things seemed to be coming out of the sky—tires and things. I had to look up in the air as well as on the track."

The most amazing thing of all was that no one was seriously hurt. Driver after driver narrowly escaped horrible injury. Driver Cale Yarborough, for example, had a piece of frisbeeing sheet metal hit him in the helmet, slicing his protective gear open, but not injuring his head. A. J. Foyt smashed a finger and bruised a knee.

Seventeen fans in the stands were hit by debris, but only one was injured badly enough to earn a trip to the hospital. But the front stretch looked like a junk yard.

The race was stopped immediately. It wouldn't start again for an hour and 20 minutes, while the mess in the approach to Turn One was cleaned up. When the race did start again, officials took no chance of further trouble. The cars took the green flag in single file.

Eleven of the 33 cars in the field would be unable to continue. Five other cars were damaged but still running. That left only 18 cars with a chance of winning. Instead of being back in the pack, Graham Hill found himself right behind the leaders when the race was restarted.

Cars continued to drop out of the race at a steady clip, mostly with engine trouble. By the 250-mile mark, only 13 cars were running. Because of the many cars dropping out of the race, there was confusion during the race about who was ahead.

Jackie Stewart, another veteran of the Grand Prix circuit, was leading until lap 191 when he had to shut down his engine, which he felt was about to blow. After that, many thought that the great Scottish driver Jimmy Clark—yet a third Grand Prix superstar—was leading the race, but when the checkered flag came out, it was Indy rookie (but Grand Prix veteran) Graham Hill, in the American Red Ball Special, who was named the victor.

When Clark tried to drive his Lotus-Ford down Victory Lane, he found that Hill was already there, kissing the beauty queen again and again. (Most drivers stop after one.)

Hill's average speed for the race was 144.317 mph, considerably lower than other Indy 500s of that era. Today, Graham Hill is perhaps best known by young people as being the father of current Formula One superstar, Damon Hill.

KING RICHARD & THE BRAWL— AMERICAN BOYS

The 1976 and 1979 Daytona 500s

Racing fans like their crashes best when they affect the outcome of the race and no one gets hurt. Such was the case at the end of the 1976 and 1979 Daytona 500s. At the 1979 race, the 125,000 fans in the stands even got to watch a fight between drivers after the crash!

Both finishes have been called among the most exciting in stock-car history, and both involved the most famous stock-car driver of them all: "King" Richard Petty. For Petty, one crash helped and one didn't.

The first 499¾ miles of the 1976 Daytona 500 were run on the smooth paved surface of the track. The final quarter-mile however, was run on grass and dirt. David Pearson in a Mercury was racing for the lead with King Richard in a Dodge on the final lap. As the cars approached

In one of the most dramatic finishes of all time, Richard Petty (left) and David Pearson (top car on the infield) bumped just as the flag man (bottom center) was about to signal the winner of the 1976 Daytona 500.

Turn Three, Petty was leading by a car length. Then Pearson went high into the turn and passed Petty on the outside. In Turn Four, the King tried to reclaim the lead by passing on the low side. Petty managed to pull alongside Pearson, but could not get past.

The cars came out of the turn and headed for the finish line side by side. The flagman stood poised atop his tower with his checkered flag in hand. Petty and Pearson were going 180 mph while only inches apart! Both drivers thought the other had the stronger car. When Pearson made his move, he didn't think he was going to be able to get around Petty. Petty, on the other hand, thought that he needed to block Pearson to save his victory.

Then they collided, hard, and both cars were sent reeling out of control.

"He hit me!" Pearson radioed to his crew.

Pearson's Mercury drifted high on the track, hit the outer wall nose first, then bounced back toward the inside of the track where it clipped Petty's car. Both cars went spinning wildly into the infield, kicking up great chunks of dirt and turf as they went. Petty's car came to a rest about 100 yards short of the finish line. His engine had stalled. The King tried and tried to get the engine started, but the battered Dodge didn't want to move.

Meanwhile, Pearson was another 50 yards up the track. His car had come to a rest near the foot of Pit Road. But Pearson's car was still running! As soon as his car began to spin, Pearson—instead of slamming on the brakes—shifted his transmission into neutral and kept his foot on the gas. (That's some quick thinking when your car is about to hit a concrete wall at

180 mph!) Pearson's alertness kept his engine running.

That didn't mean it as going to be easy for him to cross the finish line. The car was badly damaged by the crash and could only waddle along. But waddle along, it did—all the way past the man with the checkered flag.

The official results of the race say that David Pearson, a 41-year-old grandfather, won that day with an average speed of 152.181 mph. "But I was only going 15 or 20 mph when I crossed the finish line," Pearson later recalled.

Petty never did get his car started, but—since he and Pearson had been in the only two cars on the lead lap at the end—Petty was awarded second place.

After the race, Petty was asked what he was thinking during the crash. "Well, I wasn't exactly hollering 'Hooray for me,'" he said with a toothy grin. King Richard later admitted that the crash was his fault and apologized to Pearson. He then complained that Pearson had "snuck up" behind him and had hit him after the race while Petty was being interviewed by a reporter.

Three years later, in 1979, the winner of the Daytona 500 was once again changed by a last-minute crash. As the race entered its last lap, Cale Yarborough and Donnie Allison were battling for the lead, with Richard Petty running in third and Darrell Waltrip in fourth. Petty was driving against his doctor's orders as he had recently had a serious ulcer operation, leaving him with only about a third of his stomach.

Allison's Oldsmobile had been the fastest car on the track during the final 10 laps, pulling Yarborough along in his draft. There was already bad blood between Allison and Yarborough, as they had tangled earlier in the race, causing both cars to spin and lose a lap. But they had both made up the distance and it looked like it was going to be a dogfight to the finish line.

Exiting Turn Two, Yarborough tried a move called the "slingshot," in which a driver uses the suction caused by the car in front to shoot past on the inside and take the lead.

Allison, however, knew what Yarborough had in mind, and swerved to cut him off. The two began to bump on the back stretch, as they approached Donnie's brother Bobby, who was running ahead of them but a lap down. Bobby seemed to maneuver so that he too was slowing Yarborough's progress. Then both Donnie and Cale went into a spin.

Donnie Allison later said, "Cale made up his mind he would pass me low and I had my mind made up he was going to have to pass me high. When he tried to pass me low, he went off the track. He spun and hit me."

Yarborough had a different take on the incident: "It's the worst thing I've ever seen in racing. Bobby waited on us so he could block me off. The films will show it I had Donnie beat. I knew how to win the race. [The Allison brothers] doubleteamed me. My left wheels were over in the dirt and Donnie knocked me further on the dirt. I started spinning and Donnie started spinning."

The films did verify Yarborough's claim.

With the first two cars spinning off the track, Richard Petty took the lead with Darrell Waltrip right on his tail. The final quarter of a lap was just as thrilling as Petty's Oldsmobile, down at least one cylinder and not running at full capacity, tried to hold off Waltrip's desperate last-ditch

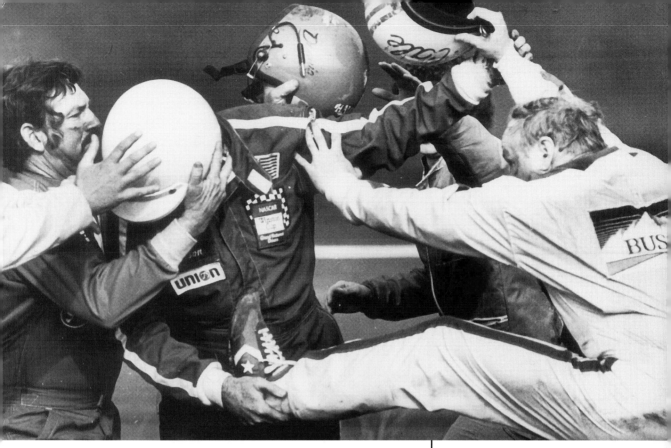

After Cale Yarborough and Bobby Allison collided on the last lap of the 1979 Daytona 500, the two started fighting on the infield. Bobby (center) has Cale's leg as Donnie (left) tries to break things up.

charge. Waltrip tried to pass on the inside but Petty blocked him off. Petty won by a whisker, but the national TV audience would have to wait for a replay to find out who won the race. That was because the cameras, as well as many of the eyes in the stands, were focused on the infield. Yarborough, fighting solo, and both Allisons, working as a tag team, had gotten out of their cars and were throwing punches and kicks at one another in the infield.

"When we came off the number-two corner after we took the checkered flag," Petty recalled. "I thought Darrell was going to come out of the car, he was so happy. He was jumping up and down and waving his arms, because he had never finished that good before. He had finished second in a fourth-place car and we were both tickled. By the time we got back around to the crash, Cale and Donnie and Bobby were out there fighting."

Donnie later said, "When Bobby came over to me to find out if we were all right, Cale went over and punched Bobby. Then he came at me and started calling me names."

Yarborough remembers it this way: "I pulled over and asked Bobby why he did it. He bowed up and I swung at him." Film shows that Yarborough had used his helmet as a weapon.

After the fighters were pulled apart, cooler heads took over, and NASCAR dished out the fines. Both Allisons and Yarborough were forced to cough up $6,000 apiece.

Did Yarborough have any doubts that he would have won the race if Donnie hadn't run him off the track?

"No doubt," Yarborough says. "And he knew it, too."

And for Richard Petty, who was in Victory Lane accepting his kiss from the beauty queen with a big "Hooray for me" grin, Lady Luck had turned in his favor.

These weren't the only famous crashes in King Richard's amazing career. One early accident led to safety improvements in stock car racing that have saved lives and injuries ever since. During a bad 1970 crash at the Darlington International Raceway, Richard's arm flopped out of the driver's-side window and was broken when his car rolled on top of it. To keep this from happening again, Petty's crew invented a soft screen to cover that window. The screen would allow air to get to the driver and keep him cool, yet it would keep all of his body parts inside the car during a crash. For many years now, NASCAR rules have required that all cars must have the driver's-side window screen.

Petty's most famous crash took place in the 1988 Daytona 500. Petty's Pontiac was coming out of Turn Four on Lap 106 when his car's rear end began to wiggle. A fraction of a second later, a Ford Thunderbird driven by Phil Barkdoll nudged Petty from behind. Spinning now, Petty was struck a second time, by A. J. Foyt's Olds. The second hit stood Petty's car up on its headlights. The Pontiac cartwheeled nose-to-tail along the outer wall several times, hitting the 10-foot screen that kept cars from flying into the crowd, then began to barrel-roll. Six times the car rolled over before coming to a stop. Shreds of sheet metal from Petty's car flew into the crowd, but luckily no fans were hurt.

King Richard's car had just come to a stop when Brett Bodine hit a piece of metal on the track, blew a tire, and crashed right into Petty. Again, King Richard was hurled out of control,

Richard Petty is taken off the field in a stretcher after his car had breathtakingly flipped seven times during the running of the 1988 Daytona 500. Amazingly, Petty suffered only a broken shoulder in the crash.

Drafting behind Bobby Unser are A. J. Foyt, Cale Yarborough, and Bobby Allison. Although they are traveling at 180 mph, only inches separate one bumper from the next. The four finished the 1975 International Race of Champions in the exact order above.

crashing yet again into the outer wall. It would take clean-up crews so long to get the track back into racing condition that 21 laps—more than 50 miles—would be run under the yellow flag before racing resumed.

Just after the crash, Petty's crew chief Dale Inman expected the worst. It didn't look like anyone could possibly live through such a violent crash.

"How you doin', buddy?" Inman asked over the radio to Petty's car—or what was left of it. Inman then held his breath, waiting for Petty to answer.

Then he heard Richard say, "I'll talk to you when I catch my breath."

Petty allowed himself to be taken by stretcher to the ambulance. But he walked from the ambulance into Halifax Medical Center in Daytona Beach. A few hours later he walked out of the hospital and joked to the press, "If there had been a long enough caution, we could have gotten back and finished the race."

As most racing fans know, King Richard Petty comes from a racing family. His father is Lee Petty, who won the very first Daytona 500 in 1958. His only son is stock-car superstar Kyle Petty.

Lee Petty, who won 54 Grand National races during his Hall-of-Fame career, endured a wild crash during the second qualifying race for the 1961 Daytona 500. He got together with Johnny Beauchamp as both cars entered one of Daytona's highly banked turns side by side. The cars slid up the track together, and together smashed right through the outer fence at the top of the track. The fence did not even slow the cars down, and both flew out of the track and crashed to the ground many feet below, outside the track completely. Petty suffered a punctured lung and a severely broken leg. He almost died from his injuries and still walks with a limp. King Richard's daddy would race again, but he had lost the will to win. Beauchamp was also severely injured in the wreck and never raced again.

Lee retired in 1963 to the Petty Enterprises garage, where he made himself useful taking a wrench to his son's car every now and again.

6

OL' RUBBERHEAD

*Rusty Wallace Goes Airborne,
Twice (1993)*

Perhaps no one in stock-car history has had more serious accidents, without serious injury, than crowd-favorite Rusty Wallace. Rusty's ability to smash up cars and walk away started early in his career and earned him the nickname "Ol' Rubberhead."

Rusty got the name after a crash in 1988. He was practicing at the Bristol International Raceway in Bristol, Tennessee when he blew a tire and rolled six times down the front stretch.

He had been knocked cold and wasn't breathing when safety crews got to the car. His neck had settled in a strange position and was cutting off his air. Once his neck was straightened he began to breathe and soon woke up.

Amazingly, he drove in the race at Bristol the next day!

But it was in 1993 that Rusty had a series of accidents that, along with once again laughing

A dazed Rusty Wallace is helped into an ambulance after his car flipped during a 1983 qualifying race at Indy.

in the face of the Grim Reaper, were spectacular enough to force NASCAR to make rules changes.

The first crash took place at the Daytona 500 on February 14, 1993. The incident started on Lap 168 when Derrike Cope clipped Michael Waltrip, sending both of those cars out of control. Waltrip smacked Wallace's Pontiac, which spun into the dirt-and-grass infield where it shot 20 feet in the air and then tumbled violently.

Ten times the car rolled over, tearing itself apart in the process, before coming to a rest on the grass. Rescue crews were stunned to find that Rusty was okay. Moving gingerly for sure, he walked to the ambulance. His only injury was a cut on the chin.

"I had a real good grip on the steering wheel when it started rolling," Wallace remembers. "I was completely awake when they cut the roof off the car."

Brett Bodine's car was damaged slightly when struck by a piece of debris from Wallace's car. Bodine moved back into the field after a short pit stop.

Wallace followed up the crash by winning four of his next seven races. Then, 11 weeks after the first accident, on May 2, 1993, it happened again, this time at the Talladega Superspeedway in Talladega, Alabama. Rusty was running in third place on the final lap, only 100 yards from the finish line, when his best buddy on the Winston Cup circuit, Dale Earnhardt, tried to slingshot past him and take away a position at the last second.

Rusty dove low to keep Dale from passing him and Earnhardt slammed into his rear end. The contact lifted Rusty's car so that it landed on its nose, crossed the finish line, and then flipped 16 times across the infield. He had taken the checkered flag while airborne, finishing in sixth place.

"After the second roll, I lost it," Wallace recalls. "I just couldn't hold onto the steering wheel anymore."

When Earnhardt and the safety crew got to the car, Wallace was again knocked cold. He didn't walk away from this one. Along with bad bump on his head, he suffered a broken wrist when his left arm flew out the window and the car rolled over on it.

Did Earnhardt have anything to say to his injured buddy? "Dale said that it was his fault, that he should have slowed down," Wallace says. "I said that it was my fault and that I shouldn't have tried to block him. Even though I got the total crap knocked out of me, it was just a racing accident. Dale would never try to hurt me. Like me, he's a family man, and we've both got too much to live for."

Accidents such as Wallace's had become more frequent, injuring popular drivers such as Davey Allison, and led to rules changes by NASCAR. Starting with the 1994 season, all Winston Cup cars were required to have "safety flaps" on their roofs.

The flaps would pop up by themselves if the car went backwards on the track or touched anything. They were designed to catch the air and keep the cars on the track rather than flying.

It was a simple innovation but it worked. The problem of flying Winston Cup cars has been all but ended.

7

COMEBACK KIDS

Ernie Irvan and Buddy Lazier

Racing's most heart-warming stories involve racers who suffered career- and life-threatening injuries in crashes, yet came back to drive again—sometimes to excel. Two of the best recent examples of this mind-boggling courage are stock-car driver Ernie Irvan and Indy-car driver Buddy Lazier.

Ernie Irvan's comeback is nothing short of a miracle. On August 20, 1994, Irvan crashed at the Michigan International Speedway while practicing for the next day's GM Goodwrench Dealers 400. Irvan had already qualified his car—the #28 Robert Yates Ford Thunderbird—for the race, and was to start in 22nd position. When the crash happened, Irvan was working with his crew on his "race setup," that is, learning how to best adjust the car's chassis for race conditions.

Ernie Irvan slams into Ricky Rudd (number 10 car) and the airborne Ricky Craven (number 41) at the 1996 Winston Select 500.

The Michigan racetrack is D-shaped. The front "straight-away" is actually a long curve. Irvan got onto the track at 8:40 AM. After a couple of trips around the circuit, Irvan radioed in to his crew that his car had "developed a push," that is, the car wanted to go right when it should have been going straight. He told his crew that he would be bringing the car into the pits for adjustments the next time around. But he never made it.

Irvan was coming out of the track's second turn when disaster struck. "Ernie was exiting Turn Two, and he headed kind of straight into the wall," said Ted Musgrave who was driving right behind Irvan. "As he was heading for the wall, the right front dipped down like he might have cut a tire. He locked up the brakes and turned a little to the left—but with the right front tire being flat at the time, the car just went straight."

The #28 car hit the wall hard—at 160 mph and slid along the wall for about 50 yards before grinding to a halt. At the point of impact, Irvan slammed against his own five-point harness. The pressure from the straps caused both of his lungs to collapse. The cross strap slid up into Irvan's neck and crushed it.

Irvan's helmet stayed on but the impact was so severe that he fractured his skull against the inside of the helmet. His face, head and neck were horribly bloodied.

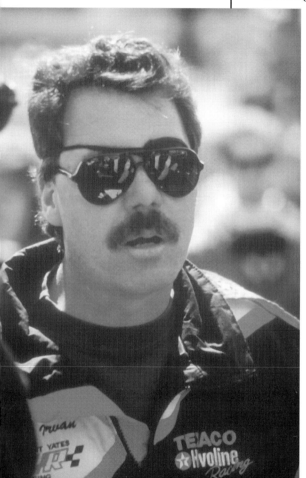

For over a year after his nearly fatal crash, Irvan wore an eye patch to correct double vision.

The injured driver was carefully pulled from his car and placed on a gurney. He was wheeled to a waiting helicopter and flown to St. Joseph's

Mercy Hospital in nearby Ypsilanti, Michigan.

There, Ernie was treated by a team of doctors headed by Dr. Greg Baldwin, who gave him only a 10 percent chance that he would live. But, Irvan is a fighter, and by Sunday his condition was improving. His lungs, which had filled with fluid following the crash, had begun to clear.

By Wednesday, Ernie opened his eyes to look at his wife, Kim, and moved his legs in answer to a doctor's command. The comeback had begun. By the beginning of September, Ernie had improved to the point where he could be taken off the critical list. He was now fully awake and his condition was improved to what the hospital called "fair."

Irvan was operated on three times on September 12, once to close up a hole that had been made by doctors in his throat to help him breathe, once to drain fluid from his ear, and again to insert a valve to keep fluid from gathering on his brain.

On September 16, Irvan was released from the Michigan hospital. He went straight to the Charlotte Rehabilitation Institute, where he took on a program to improve his strength and coordination.

Irvan put himself through many of hours of exercises designed to help his physical condition improve. His skull fractures and his lungs healed. But even after several operations, his left eye was still giving him problems. He suffered from double vision, and, because of damage to the muscles in his face, the eyelid on that eye did not blink properly. If Irvan was going to get back behind the wheel of a race car, he was going to have to do it with a patch over that eye.

It was Irvan's vision that led his fellow drivers to say privately that they were worried about his return. Both the ability to judge distances (depth perception) and the ability to see what is happening on the sides as well as straight ahead (peripheral vision) depend on having two good eyes.

Irvan, on the other hand, said that his vision was going to be no problem. During the year following his injuries, his good eye, he said, had taken up the slack for his bad eye and offered him adequate depth perception. As for seeing traffic on either side of his car, Irvan said that—like all drivers in the 1990s—he was going to depend on his track spotters, members of his crew who talk to him through his in-car radio, to keep abreast of traffic on the track.

During the summer of 1995, Irvan drove in a couple of private test sessions to make sure his driving ability had not been harmed by his injuries. He was happy with the results. He next got behind the wheel of a pickup truck for a 150-mile race in the NASCAR SuperTruck series. He led that race for 24 laps before being forced to call it quits when his truck broke down with suspension problems.

Then, 13 months and 11 days after the Michigan crash, in a moment that brought a tear to many a racing fan's eye, Irvan climbed back into his Winston Cup stock car for the Holly Farms 400 at the North Wilkesboro Speedway in North Wilkesboro, North Carolina.

It didn't take long before fans knew that Ernie was back, big time. He drove with the same lightning-quick but silky-smooth style that fans had grown used to. The crowd rose to its feet as Irvan pushed his car to the front of the pack and held the lead for 31 laps. He eventually finished sixth in the race, but he couldn't have been happier.

"It felt like I'd been doing it last week," he said.

Irvan's doctors were among those who were stunned by the speed and success of his comeback. "It's amazing how, through such a physical trauma, a gift like Ernie's skill for racing can persist," said Dr. Errol Erlandson, the surgeon who helped save Irvan's life during the days following his crash. "Given the severity of the injuries we saw, the X-rays, the physical testing at the time, I certainly would never have said that this [Irvan's return to racing] would happen. I would have been truly grateful if Ernie could have driven his wife and daughter around town. It leads me to think we don't know a great deal about what goes on in the mind and in the body."

After Irvan's sixth-place finish at North Wilkesboro, he said happily, "Everybody has asked me: 'Why do you want to come back after all you have been through?' Well, this is why. This was a ball. Racing is all I've done, all my life. I started driving a go-cart when I was eight."

When Ernie won one of the qualification races before the 1996 Daytona 500, his fellow drivers knew he was once again going to be a tough driver to beat. Irvan's comeback took its final step on July 14, 1996 when he returned to Victory Lane after taking the checkered flag in the Jiffy Lube 300 race at the New Hampshire International Speedway in Loudon, New Hampshire.

Ernie received a cool $112,625 for his victory. He finished almost five and a half seconds ahead of second-place Dale Jarrett and won with an average speed of 98.930 mph on the mile-long oval. Irvan, who had led briefly early in the race, took over the front spot with 23 laps remaining, and never looked back.

For Ernie Irvan, a comeback would no longer be necessary. He was already back. All the way.

Twenty-eight-year-old Buddy Lazier, of Vail, Colorado, was seriously injured in the second race of the Indy Racing Series season in March 1996 at the Phoenix International Raceway in Phoenix, Arizona. Lazier spun out during practice and was run into from behind by Lyn St. James. Lazier's car went up into the air and then crashed back down to the pavement.

The force of the car's crash landing broke Lazier's spine in 17 places. One fracture left him within a half-inch of being paralyzed for life. It would have made a great story if Lazier had just managed to race again. But he had bigger plans than that. On May 26, 1996, the day before Memorial Day, only a few months after his crash, Buddy was in his car on the starting grid for the Indy 500!

Lazier rode in a specially-built seat during the race designed to ease the stress on his back. Lazier took the green flag, stayed out of trouble, and pushed his way to the front. Five-hundred miles later, he won the race in the #91 Reynard-Ford with an average speed of 147.956 mph. The race speed was held down by 10 caution periods, accounting for one hour, 49 minutes and 36 seconds—or 59 laps.

In Victory Lane, Lazier struggled for a painfully long time to get out of the car, then decided to become the first driver in Indy history to do his post-victory interviews while still sitting in his car.

Lazier said that he thought his back injury actually helped him win the race: "That may have helped keep up the concentration," he said, "because you don't want to go through it again." Lazier won $1.37 million for his victory.

The worst crash at that 1996 Indy 500 came seconds after the race was over. Lazier had already taken the checkered flag when there was an accident in Turn Four behind him. Roberto Guerrero, who once was in a coma for more than a month due to an accident at the Brickyard while doing testing for a tire company, spun out in his #21 Reynard-Ford.

The car directly behind him, the #8 Lola-Ford driven by Alessandro Zampedri, plowed into the side of Guerrero's car and flew into the air. Zampedri's car sailed over the track and into the catch fence above the wall, designed to keep cars from hurtling over into the crowd. When Zampedri's car returned to the track, it landed upside down. It was then struck again by the #7 Lola-Ford driven by Eliseo Salazar from Chile. The camera being used by ABC-TV inside Salazar's car showed that Zampedri's car had flown over Salazar, who'd had to duck to avoid being hit by the flying auto.

Zampedri was seriously injured, with many broken bones in his legs and feet. He was taken to Methodist Hospital where he was operated on until midnight. Guerrero was uninjured. Salazar suffered a bruised right knee and was released from the

Buddy Lazier wears a wreath and poses in front of the Borg Warner Trophy after having won the 1996 Indy 500.

hospital on Sunday night. Zampedri underwent a second set of operations on his ankles and feet on the Tuesday following the race.

Some saw the accident as a bit of just desserts. Earlier in the race, Zampedri had been leading and had forced the second-place driver Davy Jones into the inner wall near the start finish-line, rather than let him pass. The move could have cost Jones the race, and it could have caused him serious injury.

Salazar also lost popularity with the fans earlier in the race when he seemed to veer purposefully into Arie Luyendyk's car as they exited the pits side by side. The accident damaged Luyendyk's car and took away any chance that Arie might have had of winning the race.

But the victory went to the heroic Buddy Lazier who, along with Ernie Irvan, is one of the Comeback Kids of the 1996 racing season.

SUGGESTIONS FOR FURTHER READING

Cockerham, Paul W., *NASCAR's Greatest Races.* New York: Starlog Communications International, Inc., 1994.

Golenbock, Peter, *American Zoom.* New York: Macmillan, 1993.

Hinton, Ed, "Speedy Recovery," *Sports Illustrated*, October 9, 1995.

Hymon, Steve, "Rusty Wallace," *Sports Illustrated*, June 7, 1993.

Moses, Sam, "The King's Big Crash," *Sports Illustrated*, February 22, 1988.

Ottum, Bob, "A Crazy Mixed-up 500," *Sports Illustrated*, June 6, 1966.

ABOUT THE AUTHOR

Michael Benson is the editor of *Stock Car Spectacular* and *Stock Car Superstars* magazines. He has also written *Dale Earnhardt* and *Women in Racing* for Chelsea House's Race Car Legends series. His other books include *Vintage Science Fiction Films, Ballparks of North America, Dream Teams, Who's Who in the JFK Assassination, Monster Trucks, Pickup Trucks,* and *Muscle Cars.* He is also the editor of the *Military Technical Journal.* A graduate of Hofstra University, Benson lives in Brooklyn, New York, with his wife, daughter and son.

ACKNOWLEDGMENTS: The author wishes to acknowledge the following persons and organizations, without whose help the creation of this book would have been impossible: Barry C. Altmark; Lisa, Tekla & Matthew Benson; Paul W. Cockerham, Colleen Felix, the Indianapolis Motor Speedway, Norman Jacobs, Katharine Repole; the Mid-Manhattan Library, NASCAR, Milburn Smith and José Soto.

PHOTO CREDITS: AP/Wide World Photos: 2, 26, 29, 30, 45, 47, 50, 54, 61; Bettmann Archives: 6, 10, 15; UPI/Bettmann: 19, 24, 35, 40, 48; Corbis/Bettmann: 16, 22; Archive Photos: 33; ©Barry Altmark, 56.

INDEX